ALSO BY

RHYS THOMAS

The Ruby Slippers of Oz

Eternity's Trap
The Trial of Robert E. Lee

Hotel Street Harry

Danger Close
The Rescue of ODA-525

HONOLULU HARLOT

*An Expose of Honolulu
Vice Conditions*

By JEAN O'HARA

FOREWORD

by

RHYS THOMAS

RCT Publishing

"Looking down upon her, without seeing her scarred face, one could easily have taken her for one of the most valuable women in the world."

—William Bradford Huie
The Revolt of Mamie Stover

HONOLULU HARLOT

FOREWORD

What you are about to read is a powerful little book, a pamphlet, really, a rant in actuality, laced with anger, bitter disappointment, vengeance and righteousness, yet remarkably courageous and candid for its time and subject, and clearly empowering to its extraordinary author, one Jean O'Hara, the notorious Honolulu Harlot.

Her book was written during the late summer and fall of 1944 while O'Hara awaited trial in Honolulu Circuit Court on trumped-up charges of attempted murder in the second degree, reckless driving, and driving with a suspended license.

Originally titled *My Life As A Honolulu Prostitute*, the crude mimeographed manuscript was a clear and calculated assault on the Honolulu Police Department, its Chief, and the corrupt management of Oahu's lucrative red-light district. It was so incendiary that O'Hara noted on the cover that "It had to be mimeographed because nobody dared to print it!!!!!" The five exclamation points are hers.[1] This was an angry woman.

And yet, O'Hara did find a printer—or more likely paid one—to transform her messy typewritten mimeographed document into a commercial 48 page pamphlet with a more titillating and revealing title, *Honolulu Harlot: An Expose of Honolulu Vice Conditions*. She had it printed with a three color cover and made it available right before her highly publicized trial began in November, 1944. The intent seems certain—she wanted to embarrass the Honolulu Police Department and her mortal antagonist, William A. Gabrielson, the iron-willed, hard-fisted Chief of Police.

But O'Hara's little book is more than just a rant against the Honolulu Police and Chief Gabrielson; it is a searing indictment, and peculiar celebration, of the entire prostitution racket as it existed in Honolulu before and during World War II.

Very little is known about Jean O'Hara's life other than what she tells us in her short book, and the scant information found on police blotters in Chicago Illinois, Monterey

California, and Honolulu Hawaii. If we are to believe her own words, she was born in Chicago in 1913 and reared by hard-working middle-class Irish Catholic parents who sought to give her a good education and a decent life. From her writing it's clear she had command of the English language, especially descriptive adjectives and verbs which she used liberally to eviscerate her enemies.

We are also given to believe that Jean O'Hara was her real name, though she is often referred to as Betty Jean O'Hara, and then later by her married surname, Mrs. Betty Jean Norager. Perhaps her proper Christian name was Elizabeth Jean O'Hara, which makes sense, but is only suggested here as a supposition. That is how little we really know about her and how much we have to guess.

O'Hara gives snapshots of her early life but few specifics, as you will see. She says she entered "the life," as she called prostitution, about the age of seventeen, drawn in mostly by the money but also somewhat intoxicated by the life itself. Was she a sex kitten? Maybe. Was she a lost, despairing soul? Possibly. Or was she a shrewd, fiercely independent operator who knew exactly what she wanted and how to get it? Perhaps a bit of all three. But we don't know.

Besides this little book of hers, the closest we can get to knowing Jean O'Hara is from a fictional work by William Bradford Huie, a prominent newspaperman and author of that era who specialized in getting at the truth. Huie primarily wrote non-fiction works based on inflammatory social issues. He is famous for his exposé on the murder of Emmitt Till and his scorching book *The Execution of Private Slovak*. Huie was a journalist at heart and when he wrote fiction, his plots were always torn directly from the pages of life. As he said himself, "I want to know the truth... I'm just in the business of establishing truth wherever possible. And I have to believe that the truth is good."[2]

In 1951 Huie published *The Revolt of Mamie Stover*, which told the fictional tale of a young girl from Mississippi who came to Hollywood to find her star, only to be badly scarred—literally and figuratively—and hardened by the reality

ii

of movieland casting couches. In the novel the heroine Mamie Stover becomes a somewhat willing "fallen angel" who reluctantly consigns herself to a Honolulu whorehouse and rises to become one of the richest prostitutes to ever ply the "sporting" trade. But to do so, she must buck the corrupt system and demand her rights to earn her living as she chooses. In the end, Mamie Stover is revealed as tender-hearted yet hard-boiled and strong-willed freedom fighter for herself and the two hundred or so working women of Hotel Street—Honolulu's red-light district.

If this sounds familiar it is because Mamie Stover of Mississippi might as well have been Jean O'Hara of Chicago. We know that Huie was in the Navy during World War II, and we know he served in the Pacific Theater as a prominent admiral's aide, undoubtedly spending time in Honolulu.[3] That he heard about Jean O'Hara during his war deployment is certain. That he actually met her and knew her is possible. That he read her exposé is undeniable. How else could Huie know about the Honolulu Police Department's infamous "Thirteen Articles," which regulated and controlled the women of Honolulu's vice district? Nowhere else in the literary world were the "Thirteen Articles" enumerated except in 1951, when Huie's novel was published, and previously in 1944, in O'Hara's own exposé.

We can draw certain attributes from Huie's characterization of Mamie Stover to learn more about Jean O'Hara. But his fiction is still a scant sketch of a woman who became so notorious and celebrated in such a short frame of time. The only other primary sources of record are the Honolulu Police files and contemporary newspaper accounts of her murder trial. From these we can grab at kernels of her life, but only that.

We know, for example, that she was arrested three times for prostitution prior to arriving in Hawaii. The first came in Chicago in 1934, receiving no sentence. Her second arrest was in Ottawa, Illinois in 1937, where she was tried and ordered to leave the county. Her third offense is listed in Monterey, California, where in 1938 she was tried and convicted of

iii

"vagrancy"—all prostitutes were regarded as vagrants—and given a suspended sentence of 90 days and banished from the county for two years.[4]

These accounts seem to confirm that O'Hara migrated from the mid-West to San Francisco during the formative years of her "sporting" life. Upon her banishment in 1938, we assume she came directly to Hawaii, probably as a willing conscript to one of Honolulu's quasi-legal regulated brothels.[5]

Once ensconced in the flesh trade on Hotel Street, O'Hara found the market to be lucrative but the regulations onerous. As she admits, her Irish dander often rose in open rebellion to the rules and regulations—the "Thirteen Articles"—of the Honolulu Police Department. This put her squarely in the sights of Chief Gabrielson, who ruled the Vice District with stubborn resolve and a gloved fist. She would buck his rules and he would make her pay, time and again, for the unauthorized privilege.

Seeking to escape Gabrielson's civil dictatorship, O'Hara fled to the outer islands, first to Kauai, then to Maui, where she bought three acres of land in Kihei for $2,000 and set up her own house of ill-fame without proper permission. She was immediately arrested and convicted in Wailuku, Maui, of being a "disorderly person."[6]

O'Hara persisted with her Maui house venture, eventually striking an accord with county Sheriff Clement Crowell, and later his successor, Sheriff George Larsen. As with any "accord" between Hawaii's madams and civil authorities, there was "cumshaw," the Hawaiian term for a pay-off. O'Hara knew that part of the game was the price of doing business.

Sometime during this period O'Hara violated another rule by marrying Clifford Melvin Norager, a local merchant marine who worked with an inter-island shipping outfit. It seems to have been a marriage of convenience, providing O'Hara with an anonymous legal name that she could surreptitiously use to open personal bank accounts and buy property—more rule breaking.

According to her, O'Hara stayed on Maui until late 1940, when she sold her property—getting the price she wanted, she wrote—and moved back to Honolulu. What her exact intentions were are unknown, but when she returned she checked into one of the better known Hotel Street brothels—the Rex Rooms at 1145 Smith Street. It was there, on January 4th, 1941, that she met the full force of Chief Gabrielson's wrath.

William A. Gabrielson was a no-nonsense cop from Berkeley, California, who came to Honolulu in 1932 to put some teeth into the newly formed police department. He'd been the face of the department for eight years and he wasn't about to be upstaged or embarrassed by an uppity two-bit whore, not while he was the law. Jean O'Hara, in her short time in Hawaii, had already flaunted her disregard of Gabrielson's rules and the time had come for him to chop her down.

According to police files, on January 4th, 1941, "a complaint came in from the 'Rex Rooms' where the 'proprietor' requested assistance to straighten out difficulties with one of the inmates who was the cause of trouble. The inmate, described in Booking No. 236, as a 'known prostitute and vagrant,' was charged for investigation; and then 'Assault and Battery,' Booking No. 305."[7]

The "inmate," as the police referred to all the licensed women working in the sanctioned brothels, was none other than Jean O'Hara. Chief Gabrielson sent one of his trusted henchmen to deal with her, Vice Squad Sergeant Robert Kennedy. O'Hara writes specifically and graphically of the incident in her book, so no need to recount the details here and now, but the essence was that she suffered a severe beating. A follow-up to the booking noted that "no charge was placed for vagrancy, or prostitution."[8]

The beating did not have the desired effect for the Police Department. O'Hara did not meekly acquiesce to the abuse and recede to what was considered her proper place in the hierarchy of Chief Gabrielson's Vice District. Instead she filed a $100,000 law suit against the Chief, Sergeant Kennedy, and the department. And she was represented by one of the most prominent and respected attorneys in Honolulu, a staunch, upstanding citizen litigator named O.P. Soares. He would later defend O'Hara at her murder trial.

Apparently, Soares negotiated the accord for O'Hara. A final note in the police file stated "The Rex Rooms case was dropped and the charge against the police nolle-prossed, because 'this was the best thing anyway'."[9] In the big picture, Jean O'Hara won her first skirmish with Chief Gabrielson, but she cemented an enemy for the duration of the coming war.

Over the next few months, O'Hara would be repeatedly harassed by the police, cited and fined for speeding in her convertible Lincoln Zephyr—which she owned in another clear violation of the Chief's rules. But she otherwise stayed clear of trouble and conducted her business in the brothel district without further incident, though still quietly fuming at the severe restrictions placed on the personal freedom of the girls.

That all changed on the morning of December 7th, 1941. With the bombing of Pearl Harbor and declaration of war against Japan and Germany, the Territory of Hawaii was put under martial law and all civil authority ceased to exist. Chief Gabrielson was no longer the top cop on "The Rock," as soldiers called Oahu. The new boss was the Army Provost Marshal, Major Frank Steer.

War brought big changes to Hawaii, the least of which was a subtle but significant transformation of power and privilege on Hotel Street. When the bombs dropped the prostitutes inadvertently became first responders to the wounded and dying at nearby Hickam Airfield and Pearl Harbor. The women, comfortable with male intimacy and regularly tested for VD, became nurses and vital blood donors, cooks and housekeepers.[10]

All business at the brothels was suspended and the rooms once devoted to pleasure became temporary hospital wards to house the wounded. With patients in their beds the working women had to find other places to sleep—a clear violation of Chief Gabrielson's rules. But since he was no longer in power, the women sought new housing all around Honolulu, taking up residence in some of Oahu's nicest neighborhoods.

Jean O'Hara led the charge and, predictably, she paid the highest price. In February, 1942, she rented a room at the

vi

swanky Moana Hotel on Waikiki Beach with a couple other girls—one of three Waikiki hotels that were strictly off-limits to the prostitutes. The girls had a party and things got loud. The House Detective called the police. The two other girls were evicted with no complaints. But Jean O'Hara was arrested and charged with disorderly conduct. A Provost Court judge, presumably on Chief Gabrielson's recommendation, sentenced her to six months in jail.[11]

This was the beginning of a small social war within the larger global war. The Ladies of Hotel Street, most likely encouraged by Jean O'Hara, began to aggressively assert what they deemed to be their rights as citizens of the United States, and they were backed by the might of the United States Armed Forces. Every time a girl broke a rule and the police came, the girl was supported by Army MPs and Navy SPs and the local cops were sent away. This galled Chief Gabrielson.

In a fit of frustration, and in a clear gambit, Chief Gabrielson issued Administrative Order Number 83 on May 5th, 1942, ceding full control and regulation of the brothels to the military. This, of course, was against the law. The May Act of 1941 expressly prohibited prostitution at or near any U.S. military base and made it illegal for the Army to operate brothels.

The Military Governor of Hawaii, General Delos Emmons, responded immediately, revoking the Chief's order on May 8th, returning authority to regulate the brothels to the Honolulu Police Department. This pleased the Chief—he was back in charge—but not the women of Hotel Street. The "Thirteen Articles" were back in effect, if not on paper, at least on the street.

Once again, Honolulu's finest harassed any working woman violating the Chief's rules; but they found stiff opposition among the servicemen, who were bound by loyalty and gratefulness to protect the honor of the women who had come to their aid during the darkest hours of the attack on Pearl Harbor. It all came to a steamy boil in August, 1942, when the "sporting girls" of Hotel Street did what every good working

American did when slighted by an employer—they went on strike.

For three weeks in August and September, 1942, the 200 or so prostitutes in Oahu paraded around the police station and the Iolani Palace—the seat of Hawaiian government—with picket signs. No tricks. No service. None of it was recorded for posterity. There are no photographs of the women with their picket signs, nor were the newspapers allowed to report it. But it happened nonetheless and, not so coincidentally, it happened just after Jean O'Hara was released from jail.

No one knows if she was the ring-leader of the strike. But she was, without doubt, a leader among the women and perhaps the most outspoken working girl in Hawaii.

Jean O'Hara only stood about 5 feet, 4 inches tall and weighed barely 120 pounds, but she was all heart and Irish pluck when it came to a fight for her rights and for the rights of the women she worked with. She is said to have been a tender touch for any girl in need and a fierce mama bear to anyone who threatened her cubs.

The strike finally ended when a truce was negotiated between the military and the police. The women were allowed to sleep outside the Vice District so long as they did all their business within the district. Otherwise, they retained all the rights and privileges of every U.S. Citizen. In exchange, regulatory authority was returned to the police, but their power was clearly neutered. Jean O'Hara had won another battle. But there would be more battles in this war.

While O'Hara rants about white slavery and drug abuse in the prostitution racket, what she does not write about in her expose is her role in changing the calculus of "the business" during the war. Prior to hostilities, the price of a trick was $3 and each woman often served a couple dozen men a day, spending anywhere from ten minutes to an hour with a client. But the war brought an influx of men to Hawaii that was overwhelming and the basic economics of supply and demand took over.

At first, the women began raising the price of a trick, first to $5, then $10, and $15. More popular women, such as

Jean O'Hara, could command as much as $25 a trick. That didn't sit with Provost Marshal Frank Steer, who knew that most of the enlisted men were barely earning $30 a month. So he returned the "price of meat" to $3. It was not just a recommendation—it was an order. If the women did not obey, Steer would put two MPs on the brothel door and shut them down.[12]

This presented a logistical problem. With so many servicemen in town seeking carnal pleasure—up to 30,000 on any given day—and so few working women to serve them—barely 200 in the 20 or so "hotels," and the price of a trick fixed at three dollars, how could it work? Someone came up with an idea: "Three dollars for three minutes." And that someone was probably a very business-minded Jean O'Hara.

O'Hara is also credited in some circles with another social invention: "The Bull Ring." By this, a girl would partition her room into three or four stalls and simply jump from one to the next. In one stall, a sailor would be getting undressed and washed by a maid; in another, a marine would be getting dressed and ushered out. In the third, the girl and a soldier would be getting down to three minutes of action. Using the Bull Ring, a Honolulu prostitute could service up to 100 men or more a day, usually in just a few hours time. And because it was wartime, with a strict curfew and blackout laws in effect, all business on Hotel Street was conducted during daylight hours.

So business flourished on Hotel Street during the war, and many of the working women made small fortunes, including Jean O'Hara. It's estimated that she earned somewhere near $600,000 for just a few years work.

O'Hara found other ways to make money during the war years. With the Chief's "Thirteen Articles" in the rear view mirror of her fancy car, she turned to real estate to enhance her personal fortune. She began buying houses in the better neighborhoods in the hills above Honolulu Harbor and was not shy about letting it be known who was moving in. When the neighbors found out, they often got together and bought her out at a higher price. O'Hara also bought a home of her own in the ritzy neighborhood of Pacific Heights. She did all this legally, under her married name and became quite wealthy doing so.[13]

While life under martial law presented many hardships for the average citizens of Hawaii, it was good for Jean O'Hara and her peers on Hotel Street, who lived better under the control of the military than the Honolulu Police Department. But that didn't prevent the police from exacting their pound of flesh. Madams were still coerced to pay tribute every month, the "cumshaw." Whether Chief Gabrielson knew about the regular payouts or not, it was common knowledge among the rank and file that corruption existed from the captains on down the line.[14]

Sometime in 1943 Jean O'Hara became the madam of her own brothel on Hotel Street and, quite predictably, she protested against paying cumshaw to the police. When the cops put the squeeze on her, she complained to Provost Marshal Frank Steer. Because cumshaw was nothing short of graft, he acted quickly.

"I stopped all the cumshaw," Steer said. 'I told 'em if they were found doing cumshaw they would be locked up in the military guard house."[15]

This empowered other madams to stop the payoffs, which angered the police and other silent partners receiving these shadow profits from the racket.

When the cumshaw stopped, the police response was also predictable; Jean O'Hara was HPD enemy Number One and they did everything within their limited power to make life difficult for her. She was constantly harassed, usually while driving around town, stopped and cited for minor traffic and curfew violations. She probably paid more in fines than she would have paid in tribute. But it was the principle to her. She would not be extorted by the police. And the police, in turn, would not stop harassing her.

On March 17th, 1944—St. Patrick's Day—O'Hara had a little party at her house in Pacific Heights, attended by several of her aviator friends. Sometime after curfew, the men got a rush call to get back to Hickam Airfield where they were stationed. O'Hara offered to give them a lift. On the way out she was stopped for speeding. On her return she was stopped again. This time a verbal altercation occurred and the police opened fire on O'Hara and a male passenger who had accompanied her on the drive. Fortunately for all concerned, no one was hit, but O'Hara was arrested and charged with "heedless and reckless" driving. In Provost Court she was fined $200 and her license was suspended for 12 months.[16]

Even though O'Hara knew the police were out to pinch her for even the most minor infractions, she continued to exercise what she considered to be her basic civil rights. And as long as the islands were under martial law, she likely felt that she was protected. But that didn't stop the police.

On June 18th, 1944, O'Hara found herself the victim of what she believed was a police frame-up that ultimately led to her being charged with attempted second degree murder. It began innocently enough with a going away party for O'Hara's legal husband, Clifford Norager, who had joined the military and was shipping out. The party took place in Wahiawa, just on the outskirts of Schofield Barracks and Wheeler Airfield in the hills northwest of Honolulu.

Because her license was suspended, O'Hara asked a friend, Virginia Diangson, to be her driver. O'Hara had met Virginia, presumably through the trade, just a few weeks earlier. While they weren't great friends, O'Hara had a soft spot for Virginia, who was trying to get away from her abusive husband. O'Hara had taken Virginia in and let her stay at O'Hara's Pacific Heights home.

On the night in question, a Sunday, Virginia was at the wheel of O'Hara's car driving the two women back to Pacific Heights. It was well after curfew and they were stopped twice by MPs, who heard their story and let them continue. A third stop led to a ticket for violating curfew. Soon after, as the women were approaching an intersection near O'Hara's house, Virginia spotted her husband, George Diangson, in another car. He, along with two other men, had been lying in wait for the two women.

According to court testimony, O'Hara did not want the men to know where she lived, so she told Virginia to drive back down the hill, which she did. The men followed. When they came to stop, George Diangson got out of his car and attempted to break into O'Hara's car. When thwarted, he jumped on the bumper and the hood. At the same time, George Diangson told his two friends to get the cops.

In court, Virginia said that O'Hara grabbed the wheel and stepped on the gas, knocking Diangson off the car and trapping him between the bumper and a telephone pole. But before the two women could drive away, the police arrived. All involved were brought to the station for questioning about the incident.

After giving statements, the men were let go without any citations but the women were given tickets for violating curfew. Virginia Diangson was released on $10 bail and given the keys to O'Hara's car and house. O'Hara was not released right away. Instead, she was jailed for 48 hours—the maximum allowed without filing charges. In her court testimony, she said the police told her that "this was one case I'd never get out of; this is one case they had me dead right."[17]

During her 48 hours of detention, O'Hara was not told of any further charges against her. She could only assume that she was held over for the curfew violation, and for driving with a suspended license, both minor infractions. But unbeknownst to her, the police were building a damning case against her. And they did so by compelling George Diangson to file an assault complaint against her.[18]

The police did not bring their case forward right away. If they had, the matter would have been tried in Provost Court before sympathetic military officers. Instead, they waited. All signs pointed to the end of martial law. In April, a judge had overturned the wartime suspension of the writ of *habeas corpus*. Six months later, in October, 1944, the full veil of martial law was lifted and all authority was returned to the civilian government. At nearly the same time, the military governor ordered the closing of the brothels in Honolulu. As one marine said, "the good times were over."[19]

In her book, O'Hara claims that by the time of its publication in November, 1944, she had gotten out of "the life." She was no longer a working prostitute. But now she had a serious legal matter to defend. The police had taken time to build their case against O'Hara. Three charges were filed: violating curfew, driving with a suspended license, and the most devastating, attempted murder in the second degree. And George Diangson had agreed to testify against her.

Jean O'Hara's trial opened on Tuesday, November 28, 1944. *Honolulu Advertiser* reporter Elaine Fogg was assigned to cover the trial, which was as much a social spectacle as a legal proceeding. The courthouse was packed with observers, many of them Navy officers and servicemen who were there to support the woman they regarded as a true femme fatale.

"The trial was the biggest attraction in town," said Fogg. "People were lined up at the courthouse before seven o'clock in the morning. And mostly service personnel were lined up there waiting to get in. The subject sort of intrigued everybody, and I think there were those who just sided with her, that she was getting kind of a bad deal from the police, as if they had more of a grudge against her than they did against some of the other girls. And she made the most of it. She was a very personable person, I liked her, and she was just good copy." [20]

As if part fashion show, reporter Fogg wrote detailed accounts of O'Hara's wardrobe and countenance: "Mrs. Norager appeared calm and unself-conscious as she took the defendant's chair. She wore a black dress with overlapped dark green and fuchsia bodice and black high-heeled sandals. She was hatless, and her only ornaments were a tiny cross pendant and two rings on her left hand." [21]

The trial lasted ten days, each session swelling in attendance and anticipation of whose testimony would be heard next. On the second day, the most famous man in all Hawaii, Duke Kahanamoku, sat in the gallery, along with a growing throng of military men, all enthralled with the defendant. Once again, reporter Fogg described O'Hara's visage and elegant attire:

"The striking, black-haired Mrs. Norager appeared yesterday in a black town dress with tiny bars of green down the outside of each sleeve from shoulder to hem and matching green bars down the waist back. She again wore black sandals and was hatless."[22]

On the third day, Fogg reported that "The Trial of Mrs. Betty Jean Norager, also known as Betty Jean O'Hara, picked up momentum—and additional throngs of spectators... Mrs. Norager again chose black for her courtroom appearance. This time it was a frock with a discreet arrangement of tiny black sequins over the front panel. Upon her left shoulder she wore a large cluster of orchids."[23]

The fourth day offered what everyone had been waiting for—Jean O'Hara's turn on the witness stand. Once again, Elaine Fogg began her report with another vivid account of O'Hara's apparel:

"For her courtroom appearance... Mrs. Norager wore a fitted black dress with short sleeves and deep yoke of lime green, and black accessories. Her jewelry consisted of the same cross pendant, rings and wrist watch she had worn previously..."[24]

Throughout the trial, O'Hara was represented by her longtime Honolulu attorney, O. P. Soares, who mounted a vigorous defense of his notorious yet popular client. He eviscerated the prosecution witnesses, including all those directly involved in the June 18 incident. Among the most damning admissions came from George Diangson, who when pressed by Soares admitted under oath that he had not wanted to press charges against O'Hara.[25]

In his closing remarks to the jury, Soares said, "The police, it is evident from their testimony here, were intent upon 'throwing the book' at Jean O'Hara. She herself testified that she was held 'the full 48 hours' before any charges were made against her. The complaining witness testified that the charges weren't his idea, but that of the police."[26]

Typical of the spectacle that commanded front page news every day and captivated the attention of nearly everyone on Oahu, O'Hara continued to awe spectators in court with her fashion choices on the final day of the trial:

"During the morning session she had worn another black town dress, this one with a square inset yoke of rose-beige lace with matching lace medallions on the pockets. Her shoes and bag were black." Following closing arguments, O'Hara appeared in a new outfit: "The defendant had changed into a light beige suit when she returned to the court building to await the verdict."[27]

After breaking for lunch amidst a heavy Honolulu rainstorm, the jury deliberated for all of five minutes to reach its decision: not guilty on all three counts. Mrs. Betty Jean Norager, a.k.a. Jean O'Hara, was free.

The verdict was a hard blow for Chief Gabrielson. At one point in the trial, O'Hara had even mocked their relationship under oath. Reported Fogg, "The defendant testified that after she was released from jail she went to see Police Chief W. A. Gabrielson—at this point Mr. Soares put in, 'A friend of yours?' and Mrs. Norager replied with a short laugh, 'Oh yes, a very good friend of mine'."[28]

Not only had Jean O'Hara won her case against Gabrielson, she had succeeded in her most audacious assault against him and the Honolulu Police Department by publishing her little book, her manifesto, her "Exposé of Honolulu Vice Conditions." The initial mimeographed manuscript—*My Life As A Honolulu Prostitute*—hit the streets sometime in September, 1944, while O'Hara was still under the dark cloud of the murder indictment. Her more polished version—*Honolulu Harlot*—with its three color cover, appeared in November, just before her trial began.

The result of O'Hara's exposé was significant in effecting change. By candidly telling her own story and everything she knew about the corruption that was rampant in the prostitution racket, she almost single-handedly brought down several Honolulu institutions.

The first was the prostitution business itself. Honolulu's Social Protection Committee had lobbied for years to shutter the houses of ill-fame along Hotel Street. But it was not until the public embarrassment of O'Hara's claims in *My Life* that the community as a whole rose up and demanded the brothels be closed. That happened in late September, 1944, when the governor of Hawaii finally gave the order.[29]

The second casualty was Police Chief Gabrielson himself. Under heavy scrutiny for alleged corruption in the Honolulu Police Department, and particularly in the Vice Division, Gabrielson was eventually forced to turn in his badge in May, 1946. Saving face, he accepted a job on General Douglas MacArthur's staff to help build a new police force in Tokyo.[30]

Gabrielson never regained the stature or power he had in Honolulu. In the 1950s, he returned to Northern California where he worked as a deputy sheriff for a short time. He also worked as a clerk in a plumbing supply company.[31] He died in San Luis Obispo in 1978 at the age of 92.

What became of Jean O'Hara is a mystery. After her trial, Elaine Fogg reported that O'Hara told friends "that she plans to resume study of medicine and surgery. She said she has had some study in this field and now plans to take it up for another four years to complete her course."[32]

And then Jean O'Hara vanished. One can only imagine what she did for the rest of her life. She no doubt came away from the war with a tidy fortune, perhaps enough to carry her to her final days, which are reported (without attribution) to have come in 1973. Whatever became of her, there's certain credence to William Bradford Huie's assertion that, whoever she was, Jean O'Hara was a most "valuable woman."

—Rhys Thomas
Los Angeles, 2016

HONOLULU HARLOT

By JEAN O'HARA

DEDICATION

I dedicate this humble effort to make the misspent years of my life count for something, as fair warning to young girls who are always in danger of being trapped in the White Slave Racket. I dedicate this book to warning them.

Jean O'Hara, 1944

If you will read this book, you will be pretty well prepared to follow the newspaper accounts of the lawsuits that are sure to follow its publication. Surely someone will file suit for libel against me, trying to save their face.

It ought to be fun. I have the evidence. And I have the witnesses.

Just a word in time, fine feathered friends.

And besides, what wonderful publicity!

INTRODUCTION

It is only a step from freedom, a home and the opportunity to make friends, raise a family and experience the thrill of unselfishly helping others to live, and let live.

A slavery worse than the negroes of the South ever experienced. A life so filled with insults, sordid surroundings, disgusting diseases and loathsome visitors that no attempt at portrayal can succeed in placing before you all the horrible experiences of this worst of all money rackets.

It is a thousand times ten thousand miles from the stench of the flesh pots back to a normal outlook and a useful life. This is partly caused by the fact that the White Slave Racket doesn't want to see you reform for two reasons: first, because as a Prostitute, you are a big money make, and, secondly, because you know too much and as a reformed citizen you are dangerous.

MY EARLY HOME LIFE

If you will read this book to its conclusion, you will know the truth. I was born in Chicago, Illinois, in 1913, the year preceding the first World War.. The early years of my life were happy and normal. Being the only child of a physician, I was given the best schooling in preparation for a career.

My Catholic parents were very strict in the regimentation of my life. I was permitted, however, to attend parties and movies with other children of my own age. At about the age of seventeen, I met a girl and her boy friend at one of these parties. The girl was bedecked in jewelry and clothing that had fascinated me. I immediately became interested in learning how I too, could procure such finery. I was young, easily led, and with a little psychological persuasion, I agreed to their sordid plans and went into the business of the "Oldest Profession." After the first few experiences I was completely disillusioned, and was so ashamed of myself that I did not want to go home to face my parents. Eventually my conscience partially subsided as I became accustomed to making fast money.

I LEAVE HOME

One month later, I left my home and started for San Francisco with a girl friend who was an old hand at "the trade." We started working in one of the better class houses, and I became definitely committed to the practice of prostitution. My father and mother tried every means available to frighten me into coming home, but being headstrong, and enticed by the seemingly fabulous earnings, I resisted their every attempt.

Although I actually loathed the life, my sense of shame and sin aroused in me a perverse independence. I have since regretted, many times, that I did not humble myself and go home. Again and again I planned to get away from the life of sex slavery, with all its fearful and revolting experiences. As I think back, I marvel that I withstood the abuses and shameful contacts which are an unavoidable part of the life of a prostitute.

THIRTEEN YEARS A PROSTITUTE

I was a prostitute for thirteen years. During that time I learned the history of many other girls who had taken up this life. In some cases they were seduced; in other cases bad company or professional procurers brought them in contact with the "leeches" who support the white slave racket. All the money in the world could not compensate for the insults, indignities and lustful abuse of me. I finally planned to save all of the money I could, then get out and stay out. I've known many who have tried to quit, but they eventually came back. Their general reaction is one of discouragement. They find that the public gives little help to the efforts of a prostitute wanting to return to normal, decent, and useful living.

Jobs, they are told, are unavailable for such people. The police follow them suspiciously and interfere with their employment. Consequently they are driven back to the only place they seem welcome—a sporting house. They usually lack the strength and courage to make a second seemingly useless attempt to quit.

PROSTITUTION AND VENEREAL DISEASE

Commercialized prostitution is the main source of venereal disease. From this genesis the disease spreads like cane fire. This has been loudly asserted by medical specialists and Government officials, but just as loudly denied by the prostitutes and those who share in their earnings. I can tell you, from personal experience, that the Government officials and the doctors are absolutely right. No venereal disease system of control can possibly stop prostitutes from becoming carriers in a very large percentage of cases. Over long periods of time, they infect service men by the thousands, in addition to civilians and war workers, so needed by our country.

Methods controlling these diseases by the Army and Navy authorities are probably as good as could be devised. Applying the theory that "an ounce of prevention is worth a pound of cure," prophylaxis aid stations for service personnel, and civilians alike, are provided.

These stations are situated within the immediate vicinity of the houses of prostitution. But what of the casual pickup?

Sex indulgence incubated by the commercial houses does not stop with professional prostitutes. The men thus infected, pass the disease on to "easy pickups," usually too far away from home or their aid stations for immediate preventative measures.

Thus the danger of infection is magnified tenfold. Personally, through observations and experience of my own, I have seen and say, positively, that the majority of the diseases start from the prostitutes themselves.

The venereal disease problem in Honolulu was, and is, a desperate menace to society. Methods of control and prevention, and good offices of the local board of health have been taxed to the utmost, but still the spread of diseases persist.

I want to mention some of the methods used in their all too often successful efforts to mislead health authorities as to their condition. In ordinary routine checkup, prostitutes are first subjected to a blood test; then a slide and a culture is taken, at a Central Clinic. The girl is required to wait three days before the results of the tests are made known. If the tests prove positive, the girl is sent to a hospital, where she has to stay until she is cured—a period of two weeks or more, depending on the severity of the disease. After she is pronounced cured, another series of tests are made at the Central Clinic.

This is all handled by the Vice Squad. The Vice Squad

also keeps the girls in line for their weekly examinations. Imagine taxpayers' money being spent on a Vice Squad that practically runs a harem, in the most literal sense of the word.

All results are made known to the "Madame" of the house where the girl works. Cost of the tests are borne by the girl herself. The cost is five dollars for a blood test, five dollars for a culture, and three dollars for a slide.

I will use a typical, true case to illustrate one way that all these precautions are rendered null and void by the prostitutes. A young Hawaiian-Chines girl, nineteen, who worked in one of the houses, contracted gonorrhea. She was popular with the customers, very popular, and the money she made was a source of intense satisfaction to the Madame. Both the Madame and the girl knew she was diseased, but she was kept working all the time, insidiously infecting man after man. Within a week or so, several different service men came in complaining that they had been infected.

In the same house, there was an older girl who looked very much like the diseased girl. The Madame tried to induce the second girl to bear the brunt of the complaints, and when the latter refused to do so, she was fired.

Here was an American citizen deliberately stabbing at the manpower of our country, simply to increase illegal earnings which were already incredible. A hundred or more men were infected each day during a two week period, and that meant that a thousand of more contracted the disease from this one source.

In order to mislead the health department, at the Central Clinic, the girls used to ply themselves with sulfa drug to counteract the gonorrhea germs. This they did the night before their weekly visit to the clinic. The health authorities soon got wise to this trick. They began giving other tests, in order to determine whether the sulfa drug had been taken. In order to get action, I personally reported the above case of the 19 year old girl to the Vice Squad. One would expect action, would one not? Nothing was ever done about it. Why? The Honolulu Vice Squad knows why! Soon You will learn why.

Thus it is obvious that commercialized prostitution not only incubates and spreads venereal disease inside the houses, but by advertising and increasing the habit, sex dissipation, is responsible for an unbelievable multiplication of venereal disease cases outside the houses. From prostitute, to patrol, to easy pickups – so it spreads.

In another case a girl was put to work immediately after her tests were taken. She was not allowed to wait for the required three day period. When the results came back, they were found to be positive. In the meantime, she had infected **hundreds** of men in just three days. This case was also reported to the Vice Squad. They did not take any action. Why? The Honolulu Vice Squad can tell you that there is no method of control by which prostitutes can possibly protect those they entertain.

PROSTITUTION AND JUVENILE DELINQUIENCY

Sexual delinquency cases involve very young people without parental guidance. The parents are all too often engrossed in war efforts, or in a mania for getting money fast, to bother at all. The juvenile's spare time is usually spent on the streets. In war time Honolulu, humanity from every walk and every creed of life is present. The cheap thrills are thrown squarely in the face of the youngsters who usually learn more than their share of those things, and much more than parents reared in the old-fashioned homes, can possibly suspect.

Houses of prostitution generate sex indulgence which then spread to the homes of the community-innocent—highly respectable homes.

10

I have heard of two especially appalling cases where soldiers were approached by little children. In one case, a little girl only four years or five years old pointed to dogs in the street and asked him if he would like to do what the dogs were then doing!

He said, "You shouldn't know anything about those things."

She said, "Oh, not me. My sister likes to do that!"

Have no doubt about it, these things are directly caused by commercialized sex racket in its every phase.

There are many, many local girls in this business. Usually they come from the middle class of people of this city. The kind that are just able to meet the rent; the ones that have never known abundance; the ones formerly unable to put anything in the bank more flexible than a four-bit piece. With the coming of the war, these parents started to get a taste of the big money in war work. Naturally, everyone craves attention and love, and these wayward unfortunate girls were easily influence by handsome, well dressed men, who flashed a big bank roll, owned a nice car, or showed lots of jewelry and a smooth line. These are the leeches—the "Pimps" who prey on pretty, innocent girls of this community. Some of these girls are easily lured by the promise of big money, some are led by sheer sex curiosity, and easily flattered by these smooth mannered sheiks.

Describing one of these perverted sleeklooking individuals is easy. I can spot them a mile off. I should be able to. I've seen them all—every type. The large bankroll, flashy jewelry and flashing clothing are their trademarks. They live with the prostitutes, they keep them company as common-law husbands, but there is a catch. Most of the girls are in love with these men, and they collect all of the girl's earnings. A few of the girls I've known have had Pimps beat them up if the

11

unfortunate girls did not bring in enough "takes" or earnings.

The business of procuring girls to work in the brothels, or "factories," before the war, was usually handled by the same Pimp, or "procurer." He handled nothing but the transportation of the girls, the White Slave Racket! The fee for procuring a girl from the mainland ranges from $500 to $1000 depending on the looks and the capability of the girl. Capability? The word is strength.

The Madam arranged for the money to be paid to the procurers on the mainland, who still continued to enjoy the takes of the girl while she was working here, if they were her Pimps.

During these days, a few girls have filtered in from the mainland and started working in the houses here from two to four months later. These girls signed up as wives of defense workers, and got themselves jobs in war work here. After a few months of unsatisfactory service to their employers, they were either released or discharged. There in a nutshell is the story, ironical is it may be. The government constantly has been involved, if indirectly, in transporting prostitutes from the mainland.

WHERE THE MONEY GOES

An old prostitute saying is "the woman always pays, but I'm going to make the men pay me." But it doesn't work out that way. The prostitute pays in many ways. First, she has to pay with her self-respect. She must then harden herself against the disrespect, abuse, vulgar insults and disgusting demands of her clientele, some of who are on a level with the lowest form of animal life. The fine ones, who display kindness and courtesy, cannot make up for the sexually perverted and intoxicated. Then, too, in Honolulu, the Paradise of the Pacific, grafters run rampant, and high officials are corrupt. The prostitute is also subjected to pressure every time there is a football benefit or any sort of political charity. She is charged higher fees and prices by doctors, lawyers, and landlords. Even the laundryman has his cut.

Taxes are collected by the Madame of the house, who also files the returns for them.

Finally, the prostitute pays with broken health and body. The ones that waxed old and fat in the trade during the pre-war days, were always shoved out and younger girls stepping in to take their places. Nowadays, the rush business has put even these old ones back in circulation again. I have known of a case in which the girl involved jumped over the Pali due to overwork and an over dose of dope!

In regards to the dope situation, it is a known fact that prostitution and the dope habit thrive together. I will endeavor to give you some facts regarding the dope habit in a later chapter. In addition to all of this, prostitutes support the structure of graft and blackmail, which, as you will see later, takes full advantage of the fact that it is an illegal racket.

POLICE CONTROL

At the time of this writing, I am thirty-one years old, and until 8 months ago I had been a prostitute and a madame since I was seventeen.

I am writing this book because the police controlled Vice Racket in Honolulu is rotten to the core, and should be shown in its true, unsavory light. So-called respectable business men and officials of Honolulu and the Territory of Hawaii are getting rich from the houses of prostitution, and the inmates of those houses.

I am not going to attempt to excuse myself for the kind of life I have led. I shall tell you the truth, the whole truth and nothing but the truth, and when you have finished reading this book, dear reader, a wave of nausea will engulf you.

You will react as only decent citizens should react. You will see to it that honest men are placed in power, and that the weak and the corrupt are weeded out. There is no room for them. Like the ravages of venereal disease or the crawling curse of cancer, these cankerous blights on decent society must be cut out of Honolulu city government just as fast as the axe can be made to cut their necks.

The life of a prostitute is not an easy one, and the stringent rules of the Honolulu Police Department headed by Chief of Police Gabrielson left her no more freedom than a prisoner. She was literally a football for anyone who chose to throw her around. She was a target for every cheap grafter and stand-in thief, and they took full advantage of this situation.

But yes, Honolulu is still a heaven to the prostitutes, as the earnings here cannot be touched anywhere else in the United States. By the same token, Honolulu is also a fleshmine of gold for the low down grafters.

There are over two hundred girls operating in the brothels in Honolulu. Their "lord and master" is Chief Gabrielson, and Gabrielson's orders are carried out rigidly by the Police Vice Squad. The Vice Squad is headed by a Captain in the Police Department, who sees to it that the girls stay in line and obey the rules and regulations. Further, the books of each Madame are inspected, to see just how much her "take" is. Why? You will learn about that, and also about how a house of ill-fame operates... how the girls are forced to live... methods of recruiting the girls. It does not make pretty reading. For those girls, Honolulu City Government seems worse than the most despicable of the Axis Dictatorships.

In the following paragraphs, Mr. Respectable Citizen, I will give you a few laws that you never knew existed in your fair city. Who made them? By what authority are they enforced? And believe me, these regulations are enforced—sometimes by preventing the girl from working; sometimes by the fiendishly simple expedient of beating up the transgressor, just as I was beaten.

You must know of that incident. I will tell you about it. You will not forget easily.

Chief Gabrielson ruled that we could have one day off a week, but we had no place to go. The following is a list of restrictions that we, the sporting girls, were made to follow strictly:

Could not visit Waikiki Beach at any time.

Could not patronize any bars, or the better class cafes.

Could not own any property.

Could not own an automobile.

Could not have a steady "boy friend."

Could not be seen on the streets with any man.

Could not attend any dances.

Could not visit any Army or Navy post.

Could not visit a friend's apartment at any time.

Could not be out of the brothel after ten-thirty at night.

Could not marry service personnel.

Could not wire any money to the mainland unless we first consulted the Madame.

Could not take a trip to the outside islands unless we

15

first checked out of the brothel.

Could not ride in the front seat of a taxi-cab at anytime.

Could not check out of any brothel after ten-thirty at night.

Could not check out from one house to another; we were to stay where we were put.

Could not visit the golf courses.

Could only swim at Kailua Beach.

Could not telephone the mainland unless we first consulted the Madame.

Could not ride in a taxi-cab with a man.

THE WHITE SLAVE RACKET

The Madames are women from the mainland. Before any of them can open a house, she must first get the "nod" from Chief Gabrielson. The girls are recruited from San Francisco, principally. The local "Madames" put in an order by mail, and pay $500 to $1000 for each girl, depending upon the girl's age.

The Madame, when she is notified who is coming, visits police headquarters and gives the name of the girls and the arrival date. From there, Chief Gabrielson takes over. A detective meets the boat off port and the girls are herded like cattle into the receiving station.

At the time I arrived, the receiving station was the Blaisdell Hotel. The Vice Squad was there. They explained the rules and regulations of the police department, and put strong emphasis on the fact that they, The Police Department, have all

16

out authority. In no uncertain terms, the girls were told that any violations, whatsoever, would result in banishment from the Territory. From the hotel, we were taken to the Police Department, where we were fingerprinted and photographed. Thence, we were taken to our houses to begin work. No medical examination was required at this time, and venereal diseases were rampant and sickening. We also had to have a license. That cost one dollar per year. We girls usually started to work around one p.m., and finished around 5 a.m. the next morning.

The Madame and Chief Gabrielson had an understanding. The girls were to spend only six months here, and then were to be shipped back to the mainland. Whether the girl's "record" was up to standard or not, she was not to stay any longer than six months. She got to know too much in that length of time. The girls were also under orders not to return for a year. If they did, they would be jailed. After a year had passed, the girl, if she wanted to return, would contact the Madame, who in turn would call on Chief Gabrielson and solicit his approval.

Dear Readers, would you call this a government either by or for the people? Maybe, but the scum of all people... the Gestapo of Honolulu... the dirty swindlers who prey upon women and sell every pledge; **sell every oath of office**; sell every obligation they hold to society—these men are not for the people!

Yet they walk in society, with fake semblance of respectability and responsibility, deriving much of their income from prostitutes' payoffs. Are the Prostitutes the criminals? Or, perhaps, is the Vice Squad the real criminal?

Compared to these scurvy—those officials wherever they are, who prey on the prostitute, a prostitute herself reaches the height of respectability. At least, she frankly sells herself. She breaks the law, of course, but she is neither a hypocrite nor a cheap grafter. Compared to the unspeakable monsters, the

17

Pimp is a prince to society. He plies his filthy trade—he is often a hypocrite, but, as unspeakable as it may be, he earns his money. Soon people will ask the Vice Squad questions, and they will ask them insistently.

THE DOPE HABIT FEEDS ON PROSTITUTION

I am not exaggerating when I say that fifty percent of the prostitutes are syphilitic. Thirty-three and one-third percent are narcotic addicts... opium smokers and morphine users. The fact is that along with any red light district goes dope and liquor. Madames resort to may varied measures to keep their girls from leaving them. Morphine is dope that promotes a false and high feeling. It creates indifference and disdain for everything.

Personally I have never used dope, but I could have got all I wanted. The Madames would rather their girls had the habit! Then the Madames have a hold over the girl. It was all a masterpiece of simplicity. Madames dissatisfied with the girl, could threaten the girl by threatening to cut off the girls's supply of dope. And then a girl under the influence of dope can work longer. Yes, the Madames approved of "hoppies."

There was a certain doctor who the girls went to for morphine shots. I understand he was finally caught, and was told to either stand trial or leave the Islands. He left the Islands.

As I have previously mentioned, dope is plentiful. The girls get all they want. They pay good prices for it. And rest assured that these doctors put their prices high—when the prostitute wants dope, she pays, and pays, and pays—or not a drop of grain. Morphine costs ten dollars a shot and up. How and why these doctors were not arrested for such criminal practice is beyond me, and I had a pretty good education. I did a lot of studying at one time—typing, words, writing, and as I sit here writing this I am not about to be fooled by the veneer of respect these doctors covered themselves with. The Vice Squad,

18

I venture to say, could tell you the names of these doctors.

THE RACKET

A few years ago, several Madames got together and decided to approach Chief Gabrielson. They wanted to force him to give the girls more privileges. The Madames backed down though. They were afraid that Chief Gabrielson might close them up, and some of them had only recently bought their places. They had paid as high as $50,000 for them, and discretion seemed the better part of defiance. That price, the $50,000 was only for the lease and good will.

Would you like to become a Madame? Before you can do so, you must call on chief Gabrielson, and unless you get the "nod" from him, you cannot open your place. But suppose he does not give the "nod?" You will not open. Chief Gabrielson will snap the steel trap shut before you could even say, "I was gypped."

Gabrielson still advises you (or did) to call upon attorney Fred Patterson—he will handle the lease. Leases, those for house locations, range in price from $200 per month and up, and leases are from five to ten years. Ordinarily, and for legitimate purposes, most of these places would rent for about $200 a month.

Well, you've got your lease and his approval, let's say. The next thing you need is furnishing, and then you will need expense money. Chief Gabrielson suggests that you visit Mr. Herbert Truslow, on the first floor of the Stangenwald Building, which is located on Merchant Street. Ah, but Brother Truslow is very accommodating. He will lend you any amount, and he will only charge you twenty per cent interest!

Truslow is the financial "angel" for the district. He once served time at Oahu Prison.

Don't think that Chief Gabrielson gives his approval to every girl who wants to become a Madame. Many girls I know went to him, and he gave them a curt, flat refusal. This was due to the fact that they had the reputation of being too talkative. They might not keep quiet if the Federals should try to step in and get the lowdown on prostitutes in Honolulu. So these girls soon received orders to sail. Obviously, enough, Gabrielson did not want any one operating as a Madame who would not keep quiet on the way things were run.

Chief Gabrielson would question the girl's Madame to ascertain if the girl was too talkative, or a trouble maker. Did the girl always obey all of his orders and regulations without fail? Did she know any prominent men? If she did, then she would not get his approval.

A lot depends on the Madame. If she likes you, all is well and good. If she didn't, then she could tell Chief Gabrielson anything, and he would believe her. After all, she was, in actuality, taking orders from him day after day. He considered it unlikely that he would be lied to.

The Chief likes the Madames who are quick to report rule infractions. The Madames try to stay on Gabrielson's good side. They don't want their place closed. Many of the houses are right now making a net profit of $25,000 per month. No house was permitted to have more than 30 girls. After the war, the houses would only average 10 girls. Transportation trouble.

Some of the Madames here in Honolulu are the most hard-hearted women I have ever met in my thirteen year experience. They are greedy. They are money hungry, and they drive their girls to the breaking point.

Another way the Madames contrive to keep their girls is to get them in debt. Every week or so, Pop Elie and Mickey Kane, the jewelers, used to come around with watches and diamonds, The Madame would stand good for our debts. Then

20

she would deduct payments from our future earnings.

Very few girls make under $100 a day, some of them double that and some of them make over $300 a day. It all depends upon the girl. She can make as much as she wants. There is always a line of men waiting to get into the brothels, and the Madames are slave-drivers. The price charged is $3.00 per date. Of this, the Madame gets one dollar. Out of the remaining two dollars, the girl must pay the Madame for her room and board and laundry. The Madames have a sweet racket. I know, for later I was a Madame on Maui. There the pay-off to the police department isn't as great as it is here.

Even if a girl was not feeling well, the Madame would make her continue. The Madame usually gave the excuse that she had a heavy note to meet. So the girls kept working. If she didn't the Madame might have reported her to Chief Gabrielson, and he might have given her a floater out of town.

If the members of the Vice Squad were around, the girls were not permitted, by the Madame, to mention how much she made during that day. I asked a certain Madame the reason for that, and she said, "Jean, the pay-off is so terrible here, and all of us Madames got together to see if we could cut it down a little. That is why I don't want any of the girls to mention their takes in front of the Vice Squad. It will get back to them, and then the heat will be on and we will have to pay twice as much as we have been paying."

So from then on we kept mum about how much we made. We did not even talk about it among ourselves; it was more or less, a forgotten subject.

A short time later, however, the Vice Squad started its own Gestapo investigation to ascertain each girl's take. They knew who was the most popular... the ones who made the most money and they tried to find out from these girls. I happened to be one of these girls and twice I was put through a stiff grilling.

I might add that they never did get any information from me. Twice their figures tallied close to what I had make but I gave them the wrong figure. The Madame actually hugged and kissed me after the Vice Squad had left.

For several months it was smooth sailing. Then the Madame told me that the pay-off had been increased to $100 per month for each girl. This continued for two more years, and the same Madame told me that the Vice Squad had informed her that the pay-off would be $50 per girl per month in each house. She had twenty-eight girls and pay for, so her pay-off was $1,400 per month. If it is true what she tells me, the Vice Squad collected something around $25,000 a month, there being about five hundred girls (prostitutes) in town. I hope that you are not naïve enough to believe that they kept all of that money for themselves.

At this writing, and this is Tuesday, August 29 (twenty-ninth) 1944, I understand that the pay-off is still fifty dollars per girl, per month, in each house. I also hear that this money is still collected monthly by the Vice Squad.

Once a year, the police "put the bite" on each of the houses for an additional $500 or $1000 for tickets to the police benefits, the annual football games, etc.

Also it is the policy of some members of the Vice Squad, and other police department members, to come to the houses after houses ordinarily closed, after hours, and be entertained by the girl of their choice. Formerly, when the entertainment prices were $5 per guest, the Madame then charged the girls $15 a day for room and board. When the price was reduced to $3 per guest, the Madame began charging the girls $3 per day for room and board.

PERSECUTION

But to get back to the days when I was a harlot. Betty,

22

one of my co-workers, and I decided we needed a rest. We told the Madame so. She informed us that she would have to notify the Vice Squad before we could leave. She wasn't able to contact them, so Betty and I went to Waikiki anyway. We leased a house for six months, leaving our clothes and luggage at the house. That night, the Vice Squad came to pay us a visit. They demanded that we open the door before they broke it down. When we finally did, they came in, cursed us, and told us to get back to the brothel. We explained that we had been working a full ten months, and that we both wanted and needed a rest.

They finally left, but the next morning, the owner of the house, returning our money to us, told us to move. We moved to another beach place, but a week later the Vice Squad had located us again and had told the landlord to make us move. He did. From there, we moved to a home on Pacific Heights. This time it took Gabrielson's henchmen three weeks to find us. Then they called on residents in our immediate vicinity and informed them that Betty and I were prostitutes, thereby being unfit to live around respectable people.

WE LEAVE HONOLULU

Betty and I went to Kauai, where we worked in a house for two months. The conditions on the outside Island were the same, in most respects, as those in Honolulu. From Kauai we went to Maui, where we stayed for a month. There were two houses of prostitution there, and I thought another would be in order. The people there thought so, too. At that time, Maui did not have a Chief of Police. But Maui had a Sheriff at the time, Sheriff Crowell. I was told that before I could open a house on Maui I should first get Chief Gabrielson's approval.

Betty and I returned to Honolulu and studied the situation carefully. I finally did call on Chief Gabrielson in his office, and I asked him if I could have his permission to open up on Maui.

23

He looked at me intently, with those cold, steely eyes of his, and said, "No girl in Honolulu can have my permission to open a house anywhere when she has violated my rules like you and Betty have. Who do you think you are anyway?

Then: "If you don't watch out, you'll find yourself back in San Francisco!"

Well, I have a temper—the Irish in me boiled. I told him that I'd do as I darned well pleased, that I was a citizen and a taxpayer, and that I had violated no laws. I had, I said, only violated his dictations.

TAXES FROM A KNOWN ILLEGAL RACKET

All of the girls have a Territorial tax book and a Territorial license which costs us $1 per year. We are licensed as "entertainers," not prostitutes, and what a face the title is! As you read on, its gross misrepresentation of the truth make the law look silly.

We girls are required to pay Federal income taxes as well as gross income taxes. It has been said that we girls and Madames, are the heaviest tax payers in Honolulu. That's true, if there is no holding out or cheating. Each girl in Honolulu can average from $4,000 per month to $5,000 per month, under the present day conditions, if she wants to. I have made that much and only worked 20 days a month. Many girls make more than that. So you see, if a Madame has ten girls in her house (which is the average now) and each girl averages $5,000 a month, the Madame is doing pretty well by herself.

Well, even though Chief Gabrielson wouldn't give me his O.K. for opening on Maui, I nevertheless returned there and bought three acres at Kihei, Maui. No sooner had I opened the front doors than I was arrested. I was fined $100. Two weeks

24

later, I was again arrested and that fine cost me $300.

Finally a very good friend of mine, a Federal agent, told me it was useless for me to try to operate when the police had it in for me. Well, I had an investment of more than $2,000, and I didn't intend to give up without a fight as long as they continued to let the other houses operate. Several of the girls came over from Honolulu and wanted to work in my place. Most of them had disobeyed Chief Gabrielson in one way or another, and he wouldn't let them work any longer in Honolulu.

Things eased up a bit. Every now and then we would have to take "pinches," but we didn't have to go to court. Every now and then I got a phone call from Sheriff Crowell to bring in $300 to the police department. He would call about every six weeks. The first time he gave me a receipt. This continued for the next two times. Then he sent for the receipts. He was taking no chances. That was the way I paid off the police there. That went on for a period of months, and then another house was built, in front of mine, by a harlot I used to know in Honolulu. She operated for two days and was "pinched." That was her first and last time, and apparently it was just to make it look good.

By this time Sheriff Crowell was gravely ill. He finally passed away. Soon afterward, Chief Larsen became the boss of Maui. He formerly worked for Chief Gabrielson.

Right here and now I want to say that Chief Larsen is one of the finest men I have ever met. He is fair and square. At least he was to me. However, at one time when I had decided to sell my place to a certain girl, Chief Larsen told me that I couldn't sell it for the price I wanted to ask.

"It isn't worth it," he said.

Nevertheless, the house was mine, and I finally sold it for the price I wanted for it. I returned to Honolulu. I checked into the Rex Rooms. I had been there about a week when I received a phone call from my husband who told me to get out of the house, and get out of the racket. At about eleven o'clock that night, I told the Madame that I wanted to check out, and return to my husband, and quit the racket for good. She told me that she would first have to notify the Vice Squad.

Robert Kennedy, now a Police Sergeant, was then in command. When Kennedy arrived with his Vice Squad, I was sitting at a kitchen table wearing a pair of red silk pajamas.

ASSAULT AND BATTERY

Kennedy wanted to know "what the hell" it was all about. I told him. He said that I couldn't leave until the next morning. I got up from the table and told him that I was leaving just the same. This was before the war time curfew.

Sgt. Kennedy struck me in the mouth with his fist, and the force of his blow knocked me against the wall, I reeled, stunned with pain, and he hit me several more times. How many times, I don't remember. I fell to the floor, and he kicked me in the ribs. He gave me a brutal, thorough beating.

Two cab drivers whom I had called to move my baggage were standing in the hall. They saw everything. So did Lillian Martin, who owned and operated the Rex Rooms.

I can never forget something that happened while Kennedy hit and kicked me as I lay on the floor. That she-hellion, Lillian Martin, spoke up and said: "I hope that this will be a lesson to the rest of the girls not to break Chief Gabrielson's orders! Don't try to check out after 10 o'clock at night!"

In the meantime, someone had called the patrol wagon, and Sgt. Kennedy dragged me by my hair out of the hotel. He dragged me across the sidewalk, and threw me bodily into the patrol wagon. I was held in a cell at police headquarters for three days before I finally convinced the matron that I was in a bad condition and needed medical attention. They took me to the Emergency Hospital in the patrol wagon. The doctor was an acquaintance of mine. He treated me for multiple bruises and found my body covered with black and blue marks.

There were two broken ribs on my left side, and my bridge work was also broken by the blow to the jaw. I was still wearing the red satin pajamas. I was finally allowed to contact my attorney who is O. P. Soares. He got my release from jail and we began preparing suit against Chief Gabrielson and Sgt. Kennedy.

Before I forget, let me add that Sgt. Kennedy came to my cell before I was released, and he told me that if I dared to enter any charges against him or Chief Gabrielson, I might find myself falling over the Pali someday. If I rightly understood him then, he actually threatened to kill me. He also called me all sorts of names... names that would make even a harlot, like me, blush with shame.

I was booked on three charges: (1) Resisting a police officer; (2) Assault and battery on a police officer; and (3) profanity.

Upon the advice of Mr. Soares, I had photographs taken of both my eyes and they were bery black. My right hip and arms were covered with black and blue marks.

Chief Gabrielson was in Hilo at the time, but he hurried back here. Now as to the absurdity of resisting arrest—Sgt. Kennedy is over six feet tall and weighs about 200 pounds or more. I am five feet four and weight 120 pounds!

We wanted an immediate hearing but each of the three police court Judges said their calendars were full. It was the old run around. Mr. Soares got mad and told them that he knew they wanted to hold the hearing off until my black eyes healed.

He said that it wouldn't do any good as photographs had already been taken.

Finally I was taken before a certain Judge who is noted for his square-shooting. Sgt. Kennedy was represented by attorney Fred Patterson, who told the Judge that the Police Department wanted to drop the charges against me. The Judge wanted to know why. There was no answer to that poser; but Mr. Soares and I agree to the charges being dropped. When we left the court room, we immediately filed suit against Chief Gabrielson and Sgt. Kennedy for $100,000.

Chief Gabrielson, badly upset and agitated, sent countless persons to see me and my husband. These persons urged me to drop the suit. Gabrielson called me into his office several times, and that Judas was sweeter than honey. He just oozed good will, and offered me almost anything that I wanted… even to operating a house of my own, if I so desired. I was tired of the racket and told him so.

At that time, my husband, a local boy, was employed by the Inter-Island Steam Navigation Company. Sgt. Kennedy at the time he beat me up, did not know I was married. Upon discovering that I had a husband, Kennedy visited my husband on his boat. He urged him to get me to drop all charges. My husband and Sgt. Kennedy, prior to that time, had been friends for many years. My husband told Kennedy to get off the boat, or that he would personally chuck him off. Sgt. Kennedy, was told in no uncertain terms that he had no right to keep me in a brothel when I wanted to leave the racket.

For weeks after, it was all I could do was to keep my husband from taking his gun and shooting both Chief Gabrielson and Sgt. Kennedy. Chief Gabrielson tried in every way to persuade me to drop the charges. Newspapers carried the story for several weeks. Chief Gabrielson told me that it looked terribly bad for his name to be dragged through the newspapers like that. Tough!

The Federals took notice of my case. They sent for me and wanted to know the whole story. I gave it to them. I understand they also questioned Sgt. Kennedy, and asked who gave him the orders to hold me in a house of ill-fame against my will. I understand that Sgt. Kennedy told them that the Vice Squad acts only under the orders of Chief Gabrielson, and what ever they might do, is under his orders.

The Federals told me they were willing to help me all they could, and to come and see them any time I cared to do so. Later, a special investigator from Washington, D.C. came to see me. We had several long talks. Now, don't get the idea that I am a stoolpigeon. I am not. I am sick and disgusted with the whole racket and its setup.

COERCION

In the meantime, Chief Gabrielson was still sending people to see me, and he finally sent a man, in whom I had a lot of confidence. This man pointed out that if I didn't drop the charges I would always be in hot water with the police department. Chief Gabrielson would have me picked up on the smallest infractions; he said life, living here, would be very difficult. I knew he was right, so I decided to drop the charges.

In the meantime, my Lincoln Zephyr sedan was stolen and I reported it to the police. Chief Gabrielson contacted me a few hours later and said that he would see to it that I got my car back, if I would drop the charges. I agreed. A few minutes later, a policeman came to my home. He said that Chief Gabrielson had sent him to get a note from me stating that I would drop all charges. I wrote the note, signing my name "Betty O'Hara." The policeman left, but returned a short time later, stating the Chief wanted the noted signed "Betty Jean O'Hara." So I wrote the note signing it the way he wanted. My car was returned that night. I wonder who did steal my car?

29

I talked with Chief Gabrielson on the phone after I signed the note, and told him I thought the least Sgt. Kennedy could do was to apologize to me. Chief Gabrielson said he would so instruct Sgt. Kennedy, but as yet, and that was several years back, no apologies have been forthcoming. On the contrary, he was later promoted to the job he now holds.

I knew that once I dropped the charges, Chief Gabrielson and his cohorts would have the upper hand, and would make life tough for me. I was right. I have several friends in the police department, and they tipped me off. Chief Gabrielson had issued orders that I was to be watched closely, and arrested on the slightest provocation. I had caused him too much unfavorable publicity and he was going to make it hot for me. He was either going to run me off of the Island, or get me a jail sentence.

Now let me point out something right here. There are a lot of fine men in the police department... honest men and efficient men, and if they could be sure that their jobs would be protected, they would, and could, do plenty of talking about the horrible conditions that exist here in Honolulu.

My first trouble came a few weeks later. I was charged with speeding; nevertheless, I was fined $20. When I was living in Waikiki, and there was not a sound coming from my apartment, not even radio music, the Vice Squad would break into my residence and say they had reports of a noisy party. Their manner was always abusive and their language always foul. I paid several fines for such charges, charges of which I was entirely innocent.

The police department was out to frame me. I knew it. They wanted to get rid of me because they knew that I knew too much of the set-up here, and that I again might turn on the heat.

30

WELL THIS IS IT

After the "blitz" of December 7, 1941, Chief Gabrielson started after me in a big way. he threw every shot he possibly could, always trying to make it appear that they were not coming from him. I knew better though, for friends of mine in the department would again tip me off, although it was hardly necessary.

He finally got his chance one night, while I was staying at the Moana Hotel. Two women in the room adjoining mine—the door between the rooms was open—were entertaining a couple of friends, and were dinking and feeling chatty. They were jitter-bugging. The house detective came up to see what was causing all of the noise. The women beat it to their room, closed and locked the door. I was lying on the bed reading. The house detective asked to see my identification card. He took one look at it and called the police. I was "Scarlet" Jean O'Hara... the one who had dared file suit again Chief Gabrielson. I was taken for a ride in the "BLACK MIRIAH" and the next morning I heard the Judge say "Six Months."

I served four months before I was released. That was the first time I ever did time in my life. I knew that Chief Gabrielson was the instigator. His own men told me so.

Trouble tapped me on the shoulder again, a few months ago. This time, five Army fliers, friends of my husband, visited us for a few days at our Pacific Heights home. They got a rush call to report to Hickam Field. I started driving them out to Hickam. I won't say that I wasn't speeding. I readily admit that I was going faster than I should have been. A cop stopped me for speeding, and started making out a ticked. I explained the reason for the hurry and offered to drop by the police station and pick up the ticket. But he wouldn't agree to that, so we waited until the ticket was made out. We drove off, we were stopped again by another policeman.

He yelled, "Pull over there, Jean O'Hara."

I did, and tried to explain that I had been stopped once before. He turned to the aviators and asked them what they were doing with a woman like me, a prostitute, and the famed Jean O'Hara. That got my Irish up and I drove away, letting all of the men off but one. This was, fortunately, near the Hickam Field gate. I started back to town when the same policeman pulled up in front of my car with his motorcycle.

"I dare you to hit me," he yelled.

I drove around him and kept going.

ROUGH TREATMENT

Several more policemen drove up and started firing at my car. My passenger, whom I will call "George," ducked down. The police thought they had shot him. They stopped shooting. They thought they had killed him and they were badly scared, then I pulled over.

One of them, relieved, said to George, "We thought we killed you, and were we scared! It wouldn't have made much difference if we had of killed her. She would have been just another whore out of the way and less trouble for the police department."

I was arrested on three different charges. That arrest cost me a $300 fine, the loss of my driver's license for a year, and $400 in attorney fees. Quite a nice chunk of dough for being a Good Samaritan.

I guess I was lucky at that, though, for they really were seeking to send me over the road for a good, long stretch. The thing that saved me was the Army Officer, George, riding with me in the car, who was going to be my witness. The police called upon him at his hotel. They tried to scare him off. They told him that if he did testify for me, the police department would have him busted down to a Buck Private. But George did not scare and told them so.

He was always on hand when my case was called. You see, according to law, the only time a policeman can use firearms is on a felony charge, and speeding is certainly not a felony.

Let us suppose that the police really hit George, and either killed or wounded him. I wonder how they would get out of that predicament? It certainly would have been a sizzling fireball in the hands of these men, who are supposed to uphold the law.

I GO TO THE MIDWAY

I checked into the Midway Hotel. Peggy Miller, now in San Francisco, used to own the place, but sold it for sixty grand to a Jewish woman, who called herself "Tony." There were eighteen girls there. It was a good spot and sometimes I made as much as $300 or more a day.

Tony was a drinker, and if it had not been for Hannah, her housekeeper, the place would have gone on the rocks. Hannah was getting $300 a month, and she was worth it. Later, when she got disgusted with Tony's drinking and started to quit, she was offered another $200 off record if she would stay. She was first offered a 25 percent cut in the place, but Tony later backed out on that offer.

Head of the Vice Squad then was Capt. Larsen—not the same Larsen now in Hilo. The girls were informed that they could live in either the Waikiki or Kaimuki districts, and in no other places. However, this came as a great relief for the girls, as conditions and restrictions made the surroundings, were worked in, more than sordid.

At the time I was living on Pacific Heights, Capt. Larsen came to my home and told me that I would have to move out by the following morning or quit working in the houses. I told him that as long as I was a citizen and a taxpayer, I could live where I wanted to.

A few mornings later, Tony told me to check out, as Chief Gabrielson had told her that I couldn't live on Pacific Heights and still continue at the Midway.

Tony was hitting the bottle more and more, and things became unbearable. Hannah did quit this time, and all of we girls walked out with her.

Tony was an unreasonable mercenary. She even tried to get the laundryman to mark her bills lower than they should have been, so she could save on taxes. He refused, saying he might get into trouble. However, she had put an idea into his head. You could pad the bills, as well as lower them, couldn't you? He padded them, and nicked Tony for more than a grand. Tony and a man by the name of "Jimmy," used to fix up our taxes for us girls. We never knew how many taxes we were paying or what they were for. Tony would say we owed this much or that much, and we would hand over the money.

I do know though, that she booked all of us a lot lower on our taxes than we should have been booked. And incidentally, our taxes ran in the upper brackets of three digits plus.

VICTIMS OF THIEVERY

Now, here's a pertinent question for you, dear readers and taxpayers. Are prostitutes entitled to police protection as much as you or any one else? Prostitutes are taxpayers—the heaviest.

I shall give you a few incidents to bring to light the

severe discrimination against prostitutes. About one year ago, I had a $3,000 diamond watch stolen from my home, along with $300 in cash. This was reported to the police. Nothing was ever done about it.

Again, my home was broken into, ransacked and several valuable pieces of jade were stolen. This also was a closed book. Nothing was ever done about it.

We are taxpayers, to repeat. It is a known fact that we pay some of the highest taxes in this town. Where, I ask you, are the beneficial results of our taxes?

Another example: The flood lights were stolen off my Lincoln Zephyr sedan. I reported that to the police, too, and they told me to forget about it. They said that I didn't need flood lights in Honolulu. I know of several other prostitutes whose homes were broken into, and there never was an investigation made. It shows that anything the prostitutes claimed stolen or missing, the police simply overlooked. They took the attitude that the girls always could get more, anyway. Two of the brothels also had their safes broken into and large sums of money stolen.

Honolulu has always proved a veritable gold mine for the prostitutes and the "Madames." One Madame began operating her house of ill-fame a little over a year ago. Now she has over $100,000 in property at Waikiki and she also has approximately $100,000 in jewels. Not mentioning, of course, that she paid $60,000 for her house of ill-game. She has done fairly well, hasn't she?

This paragraph may be a little off the record, but maybe it will be of help to someone in need of living quarters. War workers here are desperately in need of living quarters. Has anyone ever thought of the hotel at 154 North Hotel Street? There are at least 25 rooms there each well furnished.

The Madame who tried to open that place was very unfortunate. She opened while the Chief was on the mainland, without his approval to do so. When the Chief returned, he immediately closed her place. This place has now been vacant for the past two years. Why it hasn't been turned into a place for people to sleep, I do not know. Do you know why? The Vice Squad knows why! They can tell you the answer to that question—and to many others. But they will not.

CONCLUSION

In closing this story of my life, I waste no thoughts in regret for my misspent years. My thoughts are for the future. My ambitions are centered upon the future. My decision to write this article can be attributed to those public-spirited people who persistence in uncovering the evils of prostitution have made me see my duty. Public officials, who are violating their sworn duties, and citizens who are getting rich off the flesh mines of this city, are weak and corrupt. They should be exposed.

The cold facts presented here are intended for the welfare and interest of this city. This booklet should also prove a warning to the young girls of this community, should show them the folly of my experiences, as a result of which I am sadder and wiser today. I do not intend to preach. My only desire is to warn you that what happened to me could, under similar circumstances, happen to anyone.

Perhaps you think it odd for a former harlot to express such views, but I have quit the business. I am happier for it. My only desire now is to live a useful family life, and help others to live and let live, as one resurrected from the sordid flesh mines of humanity.

EPILOGUE

There is no use crying over spilt milk. As I have said on several occasions in this book, I do not lament for the years gone by. They are gone. I cannot bring them back. I have poured for myself a bitter potion, and indulged of it freely, and now the conventions of society are at work in an attempt to extract from me the last measure of the real stuff of life—self-pride.

You have broken others. You will not break me. Indeed, there is something in my past years to rejoice over. In my younger years, when I dreamed of a doctor's career for myself, I studied spelling, words, writing, self-expression. I can now be grateful for that. That training of former years makes it possible this day for me to bare my teeth and strike back at the loathsome beasts who preside over the gutters and the sewers of Honolulu vice.

Throughout the United States, prostitution is illegal except in the State of Nevada, and all the pimps, grafters, lawyers, doctors, and the politicians, who are picking the plums, know this. Every prostitute returning to respectable citizenship is a dangers to the Honolulu Vice Racket, Just as I am. The time is now, I lead!

I hope that you liked this book, and that you approve its intent. I swear that every word of it is true. I swear that before God. But in the brief confines of this book, there has been room for only a part or the whole story. I have mentioned only a few of the names I wanted to mention. I have finished writing a sequel to this book. It will lay the rest of the criminal ring open like a crisp biscuit.

Watch your newspapers and observe the frantic efforts that will be made to keep me from printing it. But it will be on the streets as soon as the first suit is filed against me.

End

FOOTNOTES TO FOREWORD

[1] Jean O'Hara, *My Life As A Honolulu Prostitute*. Undated, mimeographed manuscript from 1944. Original copy housed at the University of Hawaii, Manoa.

[2] Quote from an interview with William Bradford Huie, conducted by Blackside, Inc. in August, 1979, for *Eyes on the Prize: America's Civil Rights Years (1954-1965)*. Washington University Libraries, Film and Media Archive, Henry Hampton Collection.

[3] Cited from http://www.encyclopediaofalabama.org/article/h-1547; and "Mamie Stover: Blonde Ambition," by Jonathan Yardley, *Washington Post*, May 31, 2006.

[4] Beth Bailey and David Farber, *The First Strange Place: The Alchemy of Race and Sex in World War II Hawaii* (The Free Press, a division of Macmillan, Inc., 1992), p. 111; and Elaine Fogg, "Knife in Hand of Irate Spouse, Jean Norager Declares to Jury." *The Honolulu Advertiser*, December 2, 1944, p. 5. It is in this latter citation that O'Hara (aka Norager) admits under oath of being convicted of "vagrancy" in Monterey.

[5] Ibid. Bailey and Farber, *First Strange Place*, p. 112

[6] Op. cit. Elaine Fogg, "Knife in Hand..." p. 5

[7] Memorandum to The Police Commission, City and County of Honolulu, from Commissioner Houston titled "Abatement of Houses of Prostitution in the City and County of Honolulu." Undated but signed December 20, 1941, p.3. Hawaii State Archives.

[8] Ibid., p. 3

[9] Ibid., p. 3

[10] Hotel Street Harry, *Midpacifican*, August 15, 1943, p.10: "I have often wondered why the so-called better people of the town seemed to accept the ladies of the evening with little comment. I found out the other day, it was because of certain instances around here on Dec. 7th, when the HOTELS were filled with wounded, and the NURSES, who did a splendid job for them—were the LADIES on the other side of the TRACK. Hats off to them for a swell job."

[11] Op. cit. Bailey and Farber, *First Strange Place*, pp. 118-9

[12] Author's interview with Col. Frank Steer, September 12, 2001. Kailua, Oahu, Hawaii.

[13] Hotel Street Harry, *Midpacifican*, January 15, 1944, p. 8: "One of the neatest spare-time money-making tricks I've heard about recently is engaged in by one of the girls whose full-time labors take place in a local bagnio. This bright little lady buys houses, though an anonymous agent, in uppity residential districts. Then she moves in, and lets word of her profession be noised around the neighborhood. The neighbors, she tells me, always band

together and buy her house at a nice profit to her. Strikes me as a very sensible way to capitalize on your reputation."

[14] Author's interview with retired Honolulu Police Officer Chris Faria, September 11, 2001: "The prostitutes, they were paying off so much to some of these lower rank officers…Now, I am not saying that the Chief was paid off… I have no visions or never witnessed any Chief being paid off. It was always down at the lower level, from the Captain on down, that I witnessed one right after another." And, author's interview with Colonel Frank Steer, September 12, 2001: "The Chief knew what was going on… he had knowledge of it, but he wasn't getting any of the money, or what they call, the Hawaiians call 'cumshaw.'"

[15] Author's interview with Col Frank Steer, September 12, 2001, Kailua, HI

[16] Op. cit.. Jean O'Hara, *My Life…* pp. 42-44

[17] Op. cit.. Elaine Fogg, *Knife in Hand…* pp. 1, 5.

[18] Elaine Fogg, "Soares Dynamites At Diangson, In Second Day of O'Hara Trial. *Honolulu Advertiser,* November 30, 1944, pp. 1, 5. "Just before the court adjourned until 9 a.m. today, the witness said under direct questioning that prosecution of Mrs. Norager had been a 'police idea'."

[19] Author's interview with Richard Fiske, a marine corporal during the war, September 11, 2001.

[20] Author's interview with Elaine Fogg, reporter for the *Honolulu Advertiser*, September 11, 2001.

[21] Elaine Fogg, "Jean O'Hara Draws Capacity House In Judge Buck's Court," *Honolulu Advertiser*, November 29, 1944, p. 1. Uncredited photograph of Jean O'Hara exiting courthouse, November, 29, 1944, published November 30, 1944, in the *Honolulu Advertiser*, p.5, with the caption: "NEAT BUT NOT GAUDY—Mrs. Betty Jean Norager, alias Jean O'Hara, demonstrates what the well-dressed demi-mondalaine is wearing this season as she leaves Judge Carrick M. Buck's circuit court during the second day of her trial for attempted second degree murder. The trial is proving quite the social success."

[22] Op. cit.., Elaine Fogg, "Soares Dynamites," *Honolulu Advertiser,* November 30, 1944, p. 1

[23] Elaine Fogg, "Tension Rises At Murder Trial; Woman, Defense Attorney Clash," *Honolulu Advertiser*, December 1, 1944, p. 1

[24] Op. cit.., Elaine Fogg, "Knife in Hand," *Honolulu Advertiser*, December 2, 1944, p. 1

[25] Op. cit.., Elaine Fogg, "Soares Dynamites," *Honolulu Advertiser*, November 30, 1944, p. 5

[26] Elaine Fogg, "Jean Norager Freed By Jury On All Counts Of Indictment," *Honolulu Advertiser,* December 7, 1944, p. 7

[27] Ibid., Elaine Fogg, "Jean Norager Freed," *Honolulu Advertiser,* December 7, 1944, p. 1

[28] Op. cit.., Elaine Fogg, "Knife in Hand," *Honolulu Advertiser*, December 2, 1944, p. 5

[29] Letter from Ingram M. Stainback, Governor of Hawaii, to Lt. General Robert C. Richardson, Jr., Commanding General, United States Army Forces, Pacific Ocean Area, Fort Shafter, Oahu, T.H. "I have requested the Police Commission of the City and County of Honolulu to enforce strictly the laws against prostitution." September, 20, 1944. Hawaii State Archives.

[30] George Chaplin, *Presstime in Paradise: The Life and Times of the Honolulu Advertiser 1856-1995*. A Latitude 20 Book. University of Hawai'i Press, Honolulu, HA. p. 216: "Gabrielson was forced out, although the Police Commission first tried to palm it off as voluntary. Soon after he went to Tokyo to serve on General Douglas MacArthur's police staff, he was the subject of 13 local indictments alleging embezzlement, accepting bribes and other crimes, some related to a major graft operation during wartime."

[31] http://www.sdpolicemuseum.com/William-Gabrielson.html

[32] Elaine Fogg, "Jean Norager Freed," *Honolulu Advertiser*, Dec 7, 1944, p.7

Made in the USA
Middletown, DE
21 August 2018